THOMAS JEFFERSON

Patriot. Statesman. President

THE HISTORY HOUR

HISTORY

CONTENTS

❧ I ❧

INTRODUCTION

"One man with courage is a majority."

— THOMAS JEFFERSON

❧❧❧

Founding father. Patriot. Statesman. President.

❧❧❧

Thomas Jefferson was all of these things and more. He was one of the men who helped to bring the United States into being, and he shepherded the country through some of the most dynamic political years in its history. It is very possible that without his brilliance, the fledgling democracy, the first in the world since the end of Ancient Greece, may not have survived its first few trials by fire.

❦

Jefferson was a great man. He was also a complicated man and a man whose moral convictions were unwavering in some areas and completely conflicted in others.

❦

To many of us, he is like a statue, a perfect image of a man frozen in marble. Look more closely, though, and you can see that the statue has feet of clay.

✢ II ✢

BORN TO PRIVILEGE

"I like the dreams of the future better than the history of the past."

— THOMAS JEFFERSON

✶

Thomas Jefferson was born on April 13, 1743, as a subject of the British Crown. He was the third of ten children of Peter Jefferson and Jane Randolph, who at the time of his birth lived at Shadwell in the Colony of Virginia, in the shadow of the Blue Ridge Mountains. He was part of the well-to-do elite. Peter Jefferson was a planter and surveyor in the County of Albemarle. His mother was the daughter of Isham Randolph, a sea captain who was the son of William Randolph, one of the wealthiest planters in all of Virginia.

Theirs was a large family, as was normal at the time: Jane, who would die a spinster; Mary, who would marry a member of the Virginia House of Burgesses; Thomas Jefferson himself; Elizabeth; Martha, who would marry Jefferson's best friend, Dabney Carr; two boys named Peter, both of whom died in infancy; Lucy; and lastly the twins, Anna and Randolph.

EARLY EDUCATION

※

In 1745, Colonel William Randolph, Jane Randolph Jefferson's grandfather, and Peter Jefferson's close friend passed away, leaving Peter as the executor of his estate and the guardian of his infant son, Jefferson Mann Randolph. The estate that Randolph left behind was a plantation called Tuckahoe. In order to attend to his new duties, Peter relocated the family from Shadwell to Tuckahoe. Thomas Jefferson later recorded that his first memory arose from this time when he recalled being carried on a pillow by a slave during the family's move. Slavery would shadow Jefferson until the end of his life.

※

While he was at Tuckahoe, Jefferson began his education with private tutors. His father regretted never having had a proper education of his own, so he pushed young Jefferson, his first-born son, to enter school early. He began his studies at the tender age of five years old.

❦

The family returned to Shadwell in 1752, when Jefferson was nine years old. He was enrolled in a local school run by a Presbyterian minister from Scotland. His learning incorporated Latin, Greek and French, and he began to study the natural world, which would remain a lifelong passion. He also learned horseback riding and spent many hours reading the books in his father's library.

❦

In 1758, his tutelage passed to Reverend James Maury, who ran a boarding school near Gordonsville, Virginia. It was not a boarding school in the traditional sense; rather, Reverend Maury hosted the children that he taught, and they lived in his home with his family. Here, he added history, science, music and the classics (Cicero, Homer, Plato, and Aristotle among them) to his curriculum. He traveled to Williamsburg with Reverend Maury and met Patrick Henry, the future patriot, who was eight years old than Jefferson but whom he came to like a great deal unless they were arguing against one another in court. The two bonded over their common love of music, specifically the violin, which they both played. He stayed with Maury for two years, returning to Shadwell in 1760.

❦

At that time, Virginia was on the frontier, and Jefferson came to know many Native American traders who stopped over at

Shadwell while they were traveling to Williamsburg for business. Among these Native Americans was the Cherokee chief Ontassete. When Chief Ontassete took his leave of his people before he made the perilous trip to London, Jefferson was in attendance. The chief's oratory and the connection he had with his people moved him, and he vowed that he would try to emulate the chief's eloquent example.

INHERITANCE AND MORE
LEARNING

❦

W hen Jefferson was only 14 years old, his father died, leaving his estate to be divided between Jefferson and his brother, Randolph. Jefferson's share of the inheritance was about 5,000 acres of land and between 20 and 40 slaves. He was able to take full command of the property once he turned 21. Despite the beauty of the place and lucrative nature of the inheritance, he dreamed of living on a mountain.

❦

When he was 16 years old, only two years after his father's death, Jefferson entered the College of William and Mary in Williamsburg. His professor, William Small, taught him mathematics, metaphysics, and philosophy, and he introduced him to some of the premier minds of his day. These included George Wythe, a brilliant law professor, and Francis Fauquier, the Lieutenant Governor of Virginia Colony. Fauquier used to throw lavish parties, and Jefferson was invited to them all, where he would play the violin, flirt with ladies and drink expensive, imported wine. More serious companions were British Empiricists and philosophers like John Locke, Francis Bacon, and Isaac Newton, all of whom had a strong influence on Jefferson. He was befriended and invited into their inner circle, and on Friday nights he and these learned men would gather to discuss politics and philosophical questions of the day.

⚜

Although he was much impressed by geniuses around him, he was still a young man, and he wasted much time and money in his first year at the college on the parties that Fauquier would throw. He quickly regretted his profligacy and dedicated himself to rigorous study at the beginning of his second year. He would study for fourteen hours every day, and his skills at French, Greek, and the violin improved immensely. He graduated in 1762 after only two years.

⚜

He took work as a law clerk in the office of Professor Wythe, who taught him the law and helped him to obtain his law license. Jefferson was always a voracious reader, and he read English classics, political treatises, law, philosophy, history, natural law, *"**natural religion**,"* ethics, architecture, botany, and agriculture. Professor Wythe was so impressed by his intellect and driven curiosity that when he died, he bequeathed his entire library to Jefferson. His love of reading was a quality he never lost, and in later years, he stated,

"I cannot live without books."

LAWYER AND POLITICIAN

❦

Jefferson became a licensed attorney in 1767 after he passed the Virginia bar. He also began his political career, representing the county of Albemarle in the Virginia House of Burgesses, one of the houses of civilian government in the colony. He served from 1769 until 1775.

❦

Among Jefferson's efforts in the House of Burgesses were a series of attempts to reform slavery. In the colonies, the Governor of Virginia and the Royal Court had the last word on the emancipation of slaves. In 1769, he introduced legislation to change that. He wanted masters to have the right to emancipate their slaves as they wished, and even persuaded his cousin, Richard Bland, to join him in attempting to pass the bill. The Burgesses' reaction was strongly negative, and the law was never passed.

He turned instead to his legal practice, where he accepted several cases for slaves seeking freedom, which he took on pro bono, meaning he waived his fee. While arguing for the freedom of one client, who sought emancipation while he was still technically too young by law, Jefferson made his first argument in support of individual rights and personal liberty, which he stated were granted by God as part of Natural Law. The judge in the case refused to let him finish his statement and summarily ruled against his client. In response, Jefferson gave his enslaved client a large sum of money, and the client mysteriously vanished, heading north with Jefferson's assistance.

He had several notable cases that he argued before the highest court in the colony: *Howell v Netherland* (1770), in which he stated that all human beings are born free; *Bolling v Bolling* (1771), during which he and his old law professor Wythe argued for opposite sides; and *Blair v Blair* (1772), a scandalous divorce case that had such flagrantly sexual content that Jefferson's notes called the evidence "***voluminous and indecent.***" Legal scholars have called the Blair case the baby steps of the ideas of liberty that led to American independence.

❧ III ❧

MARRIAGE AND
MONTICELLO

"The happiest moments of my life have been the few which I have passed at home in the bosom of my family."

— THOMAS JEFFERSON

❦

Jefferson had long wished to live on a mountain, and in his boyhood, he had spent many happy days playing on the 868-foot mountain that stood above his home in Shadwell. He named the mountain Monticello. In 1768, Jefferson hired workers and deployed his slaves to clear a 250 square foot patch of ground on the highest point of that mountain, and for the next forty years, he would design, build, tear down, and rebuild the house until it became the architectural showpiece that still stands today.

The first structure of Monticello was a small, single-room brick house with a walk-out basement and workshop. This came to be known as the South Pavilion, and in 1770, he took up residence in the house, which he had designed from the ground up, and which overlooked his 5,000-acre plantation.

MARRIAGE, FAMILY, AND
SORROW

༺❀༻

On January 1, 1772, Thomas Jefferson married Martha Wayles Skelton, his 23-year-old widowed third cousin. She was a gifted household manager, a glittering hostess and blessed with both intellect and musical skill. She was an accomplished pianist, and Jefferson would often accompany her on violin or cello. She was also renowned for the delicacy and skill of her needlework. The years of their marriage were the happiest of Thomas's life, and together they had six children, only two of whom lived to adulthood: Martha, called Patsy; Jane, who lived only one year; a son who died nameless after two weeks; Mary Wayles, called Polly; Lucy Elizabeth, who died after one year; and another daughter named Lucy Elizabeth, who only lived for three years. Patsy and Polly were the only survivors, and though this was tragic, it was not terribly unusual for the time.

༺❀༻

Martha's father died in 1773, and the couple inherited 135 slaves, including Martha's half-sister Sally Hemings. Under the law, any child born to an enslaved mother was herself automatically enslaved, and though Sally was as cultured, intelligent and educated as Martha, she remained a slave until her death. Future years would see Sally and Thomas Jefferson extremely close, and the controversy around their relationship survives to this day.

❦

In addition to humans in bondage, Martha and Thomas also inherited an estate, a slave-trading business, and a mountain of debt. It took Jefferson years of effort to settle his late father-in-law's business liabilities, but he paid off everyone.

❦

Martha was not a strong woman, nor a healthy one; her mother had died quite young, and she had endured difficult relationships with two stepmothers. During the ten years of their marriage, Martha bore many children, and with each pregnancy, her health declined. She died on September 6, 1782, only a few months after the birth of the last Lucy Elizabeth, with Jefferson at her bedside. Before her death, she made him swear to never remarry because she didn't want her daughters to suffer at the hands of a stepmother as she had done. He swore the oath as she requested.

❦

Jefferson was nearly undone by his wife's death. He would spend long, grief-stricken nights pacing and weeping until he nearly dropped from exhaustion. He would take long, aimless rides with Patsy, and though he tried to conceal his suffering from his children, he would sometimes suffer "*violent bursts of grief.*" Some who knew him said that he never stopped grieving for his "*cherished companion.*"

RETURN TO POLITICS

※

On December 16, 1773, a group of radical separatists calling themselves the Sons of Liberty boarded a ship in Boston Harbor that belonged to the British East India Tea Company. They were acting in opposition to the Townsend Acts, a set of laws passed by Parliament to undercut Colonial businesses in favor of companies based in Britain. Dressed as Native Americans, they tossed crates of tea overboard, destroying the entire valuable cargo. In retaliation, Parliament passed what came to be called the Intolerable Acts in 1774.

※

Until these acts had passed, Massachusetts Colony had enjoyed a marked degree of autonomy and self-governance. These rights were granted by the Massachusetts Charter, which was revoked by the Intolerable Acts. The Acts also closed Boston Harbor to shipping until the Colonists paid reparations for the ruined tea shipment, effectively denying Boston merchants the right to trade. The acts were meant to punish Massachusetts for the actions of the Sons of Liberty, with the intention of forcing the wayward colony back into line. In response to these punitive measures, the colonists formed the First Continental Congress, and a body made up of representatives from all thirteen colonies which met in Philadelphia to determine their future course of action.

❧

Jefferson wrote a resolution calling for a day of fasting and prayer and arguing that the people have the right to govern themselves. He also called for a boycott of all goods from Britain. He published his resolution under the title *A Summary View of the Rights of British America*. This treatise was presented to *the First Continental Congress* as a list of grievances against King George III and his government.

❧

The Continental Congress forwarded their grievances to the king as a petition for change. The petition was ignored. The *Summary* was printed in pamphlet form and distributed widely in London, New York, and Philadelphia, which earned him a reputation as a skillful, persuasive and radical political thinker.

❦ IV ❦

REVOLUTION AND NATION BUILDING

"We hold these truths to be self-evident: that all men are created equal; that they are endowed by their Creator with certain unalienable rights; that among these are life, liberty and the pursuit of happiness."

— THOMAS JEFFERSON

❦

The lack of an acceptable response to their petition drove the colonists to convene a Second Continental Congress in 1775. This time, instead of trying to find a way to reconcile with their royal master in London, the colonists turned their attention to independence. They issued the Lee Resolution, which declared that the United Colonies were independent from Britain. The formal political revolution had begun.

DECLARATION OF
INDEPENDENCE

꧁꧂

In July 1776, the Colonies had been at war with Great Britain for almost a year, with the first battles being fought at Lexington and Concord in 1775. Despite the open hostilities, many colonists were still hoping that there might be some form of reconciliation with the Crown. When Parliament passed the Prohibitory Act in February 1776, which blockaded American ports and declared all American ships to be enemy vessels, the Massachusetts pro-independence firebrand John Adams stated that Parliament had already declared American independence and that it was time for the British Empire to be dismantled.

꧁꧂

Many Americans agreed. There were fully ninety different declarations of independence that circulated throughout the colonies, but there were none that every colony endorsed. The colonies were declaring themselves independent in a piecemeal fashion, but there needed to be a more uniform document to which all of the colonies agreed.

❦❧❦

Jefferson, one of the youngest delegates to the Second Continental Congress at 33 years old, was included in the Committee of Five, which was formed to draft a declaration of independence. Another member of the Committee of Five was John Adams, who would become one of Jefferson's closest friends and bitterest political rivals.

❦❧❦

The Committee of Five worked on the draft of the Declaration for seventeen days, with Jefferson doing most of the writing. He believed that Adams should be the principal author of the Declaration, but Adams pushed tor Jefferson to take the lead. He drew from a proposed draft of the Virginia Constitution that he had written as well as from the Virginia Declaration of Rights by George Mason. The other committee members made a few changes, and the finished draft was provided on June 28, 1776.

❦❧❦

Congress tinkered with the Declaration for two long days, arguing vehemently about what should and should not be included. There was a long passage that was deeply critical of the slave trade, claiming that Britain had forced the institution onto the colonies. The delegates from the southern colonies were all planters and slave owners, and after two days of debate, the passage was struck from the final document. The slavery passage was omitted so that the document would appear less radical, thereby not offending some individuals in the British Parliament who were secretly supportive of American independence. Jefferson never spoke publicly about the revisions, but he personally resented the changes that were imposed upon his document. He wrote privately that Congress had "***mangled***" his draft.

⚘

The Congress ratified the Declaration of Independence on July 4, 1776, and all of the delegates signed it on August 2, 1776. There is a legend, possibly apocryphal, that when John Hancock placed his famously large-sized signature on the document, he said, urging unity of action,

> *"Now we must all hang together."*

Benjamin Franklin supposedly responded,

> *"Yes, we must indeed all hang together, or most assuredly we shall all hang separately."*

The act of signing the document was an act of treason against King George, and they all knew that if the revolution failed, their lives would be forfeit. Jefferson and his fellows showed great bravery in openly defying their imperial master.

THE STATE OF VIRGINIA

❦

When the revolution began, Jefferson held the rank of Colonel and was appointed the commander of the Albemarle County Militia. Almost immediately, in September 1776, he was elected to the Virginia House of Delegates to represent his county. For three years, he concentrated on writing the constitution for the State of Virginia. He entered legislation called the Bill for Establishing Religious Freedom, which prohibited state support or enforcement of religious institutions or beliefs. He also entered a bill seeking to disestablish the Anglican Church in Virginia. Both bills failed to pass.

❦

As one of the pre-eminent legal minds in the state, Jefferson was tasked with revising the entire corpus of Virginia's laws. He wrote 126 bills in three years, a monumental achievement and effort. His laws reformed the judicial system established requirements for standardized general education and attacked the "*feudal*" system of primogeniture which had dominated inheritance laws.

৩৯৩

Jefferson was elected as Governor of Virginia in 1779 and 1780, serving two one-year terms. During his tenure, he transferred the state capital from Williamsburg to Richmond and continued his work to reform and promote education, freedom of religion and revised inheritance laws.

৩৯৩

He was in Richmond when British forces marched on the city under the command of traitor Benedict Arnold, and he narrowly escaped with his life when the enemy burned the city to the ground. He was the target of a cavalry detachment sent by British General Charles Cornwallis, and he and other members of the Virginia General Assembly would have been captured had it not been for the intervention of Jack Jouett and the Virginia Militia. He took refuge his second plantation, Poplar Forest. There were suggestions that he had acted with cowardice, but an inquest by the Assembly determined that he had acted with honor.

৩৯৩

Jefferson received a letter from French diplomat François Barbé-Marbois in 1780, asking about the geography, history, and government of Virginia. He published his response in a book called *Notes on the State of Virginia*. Over the course of five years, he wrote an exhaustive study of his state, including reviews of scientific knowledge, history, politics, state law, natural resources, economy, culture, and geography. He also commented at length on slavery and miscegenation (mixing of the races). He believed that blacks and whites would never be able to coexist as free people because of the depth of resentment that would necessarily and rightly be caused by the institution of slavery.

⊗

The book was first published in French in 1785, and an English language version was published in 1787. It was hailed as a great achievement and is still much respected, believed by many to be the most important American book published before 1800.

CONGRESS AND FOREIGN
AFFAIRS

༺༝༛

A fter the capitulation of the British army and the peace treaty that followed, the newborn United States formed a Congress of the Confederation. Jefferson was the delegate from Virginia. He joined a committee dedicated to setting foreign exchange rates, and it was his suggestion that American currency be based on the decimal system.

༺༝༛

Jefferson was chairman of a committee that was dedicated to establishing a new system of government for the nation, as well as to determine a standard set of rules for the settlement of western territories. The committee met during the 1783-1784 session of Congress. Jefferson proposed that Virginia should cede to the national government all of the territory it had claimed in the Ohio River basin, with the condition that the territory should be sectioned into areas that could in time become new states. He also suggested that slavery should be banned in all of the nation's territories. This bill was called the Land Ordinance of 1784, and it underwent a great deal of revision by Congress, including the elimination of the anti-slavery provision. This provision, called the "**Jefferson Proviso**," was incorporated into the Northwest Ordinance of 1787.

⚜

The Congress of the Confederation sent Jefferson to join Benjamin Franklin and John Adams in Europe, where he would work to negotiate trade agreements with England, Spain, and France. He spent five years in Paris as Minister to France, and his work there helped to shape the United States' foreign policy. He traveled to France with his daughter Patsy and two servants, including James Hemings, a slave and the older brother of Sally Hemings. He had James trained in the ways of French cooking, and he sent Patsy to be educated at the Pentemont Abbey.

⚜

In 1786, he had a torrid six-week affair with Maria Cosway, an English/Italian musician. They were together frequently, but Maria had a husband. The affair ended when she returned to England, but the two continued to correspond for the rest of their lives.

⚜

Jefferson sent for his daughter Patsy in June 1787, and she was accompanied by Sally Hemings, who was at that time 16 years old. While in Paris, it is believed that Jefferson and Sally began a sexual relationship, during which she became pregnant. According to an account written later by Sally's son Madison, she agreed to return to the United States on the condition that Jefferson would free her children when they reached the age of majority.

❧

During his stay in France, Jefferson became close friends with the Marquis de Lafayette, who had come to the aid of the colonies during the American revolution. The Marquis helped Jefferson to obtain trade agreements with the French crown. Jefferson was a supporter of the French Revolution, although he was uncomfortable with the more violent aspects of the undertaking. He was in Paris when revolutionaries stormed the Bastille, and he allowed the Marquis de Lafayette and his republican allies to meet at his residence. When the Marquis was writing the *Declaration of the Rights of Man and the Citizen*, Jefferson consulted with him and helped him draft the document.

SECRETARY OF STATE

❦

Jefferson returned to the United States in 1789 and accepted President George Washington's invitation to serve as Secretary of State. At that time, the two items of greatest concern were the national debt and the location of the capital.

❦

Jefferson believed that each state should be responsible for its debt, which put him in direct conflict with Alexander Hamilton, Secretary of the Treasury, who favored the consolidation of the states' debts into one debt held by the federal government. Hamilton was also dedicated to the establishment of a national bank, which Jefferson also opposed. He did everything he could to undermine Hamilton's plans, which so angered Washington that he nearly dismissed Jefferson from the cabinet.

⚜

Jefferson and Hamilton sparred over the location of the capital, as well. Hamilton wanted to situate the capital in the Northeast, near the cities that formed the center of commerce in the fledgling nation. Jefferson, Washington and other members of the planter elite wanted the capital further to the south. The Compromise of 1790 settled the argument, with the capital being located on the banks of the Potomac River and the national government taking on the war debts of all of the states.

⚜

In May 1792, Jefferson took umbrage at the developing political rivalries that he saw forming, and he wrote to Washington asking him to run for re-election, hoping that the great man would be a stabilizing influence. He wanted to create a political party to counter the Federalists, who were led by Alexander Hamilton. Jefferson espoused a position that would become the platform of the Democratic-Republican Party, which sought to increase states' rights and to oppose the sort of centralization of power that the Federalists pursued.

⚜

While he was a member of Washington's cabinet, he was an enthusiastic supporter of France. When France and Britain entered into conflict in 1793, he pushed for the United States to support France against her enemy. His efforts were undermined by the antipathy that the French Revolutionary ambassador, Edmond-Charles Genêt, showed to President Washington.

The interpersonal and political in-fighting caused Jefferson to develop migraines and garnered resentment from Washington. In December 1793, Jefferson resigned his cabinet position. Washington never forgave him, and the two men never spoke again. The animosity between the two was so great that when Washington died in 1799, Jefferson chose to remain at Monticello rather than attending his funeral.

❦

In 1794, Washington negotiated the Jay Treaty with Great Britain. The treaty was largely authored by Alexander Hamilton and formed an agreement whereby Britain relinquished territories in the Northwest that it had claimed in violation of the post-revolution peace treaty (the Treaty of Paris) in return for increased trade between the two countries. Jefferson saw this treaty as a serious overreach on the part of Jay and Hamilton, and he warned that it would undermine the republic and unduly increase Britain's influence. From Monticello, he organized a national resistance to the treaty, which became the Democratic-Republican Party.

ELECTION OF 1796

꧁꧂

Jefferson ran for president in 1796 on the Democratic-Republican ticket, running against John Adams of the Federalist Party. He lost in the electoral college, but because of a quirk in the proceedings, he won the position of Vice President. He became the presiding officer of the Senate, but he limited his participation to issues of procedure, allowing the Senators to debate as they wished.

꧁꧂

While he was Vice President, during the spring of 1797, Jefferson met four times with French consul Joseph Létombe. He attacked and undermined Adams and encouraged France to invade England. He also advised Létombe to stall any and all envoys to Paris sent by the Adams administration, which resulted in an openly hostile approach to the sitting president. Adams sent peace envoys to Paris, but they were rebuffed, an embarrassment that led Jefferson and his fellows to call for a release of all documents related to the issue. Unfortunately, this backfired, as the documents revealed that French officials had demanded bribes. The incident, called the XYZ Affair, turned public opinion against France and led to an undeclared war between the two countries called the Quasi-War.

⚜

The Adams administration passed the Alien and Sedition Acts, which Jefferson believed were both unconstitutional and aimed at suppressing his party. With the assistance of James Madison, he anonymously wrote the Kentucky and Virginia Resolutions. These resolutions permitted states to protect their citizens from federal laws that they believed were unconstitutional, something called interposition. Jefferson also advocated nullification, which was the right of states to invalidate objectionable federal laws completely. Washington was horrified by these resolutions, correctly recognizing in them the seed of future disunion. Nullification and interposition contributed to the American Civil War.

⚜

Jefferson and Madison moved to Philadelphia in 1791 and founded the *National Gazette*, which was meant to directly counter the Federalist newspaper the *Gazette of the United States*, which had been created by Jefferson's old adversary, Alexander Hamilton. The *National Gazette* ran pieces by "Brutus" (James Madison) that sharply criticized Hamilton's policies and ideas. It was a war of words.

❧ V ☙
PRESIDENCY

"Politics is such a torment that I advise everyone I love not to mix with it."

— THOMAS JEFFERSON

☙❧

The 1800 Presidential election was one of the most heated and hateful affairs in all of American history. Jefferson ran once again at the head of the Democratic-Republican ticket, opposed by John Adams, who was seeking re-election. The incumbent was weakened by unpopular taxes and political backlash over the Quasi-War with France. Jefferson accused the Federalists of being secret monarchists; Adams accused Jefferson of being a libertine who was under the control of the French.

Ultimately, the Democratic-Republicans won more electoral college votes, but Jefferson and his running mate Aaron Burr received exactly the same number of votes in total. The election was decided by the House of Representatives, which was dominated by the Federalists. Alexander Hamilton unexpectedly argued in favor of a Jefferson win, relegating Burr to the office of vice president. Jefferson won the election.

When Adams had come to power, his administration had included many of the same people who had served under Washington, since Washington's people and Adams were all Federalists. Jefferson's administration would be drawn from his Democratic-Republican party faithful, with an almost wholesale reseating of the officers of government. This was accomplished with no violence and no strife. The election of 1800 was the first peaceful transition from one political party to another in American history.

CHIEF EXECUTIVE

❦

J efferson was sworn in on March 4, 1801, by Supreme
Court Chief Justice John Marshall. Unlike his predeces-
sors, Jefferson had no taste for formality or pomp. He
rode to the inauguration on horseback, taking his horse
to the stable himself. He was dressed plainly and came
without any escort. His inaugural address stressed reconciliation with the Federalists, and his cabinet was made up of
moderates. He was a fiercely political animal, but he came to
Washington willing to work with the other side on behalf of
the people.

❦

The nation was burdened with an $83 million debt when he
came into office. With the help of his Secretary of the Treasury Albert Gallatin, he set about dismantling Hamilton's
fiscal system and tried to disassemble the national bank. He
eliminated a tax on whiskey, closed what he called "***unneces-***

sary offices" and reduced the Navy on the grounds that it wasn't needed in peacetime. He turned the Navy into a fleet of cheap gunboats that were useful only in defense, believing that this would not provoke any hostility from foreign powers. By the end of his second term, he had reduced the debt from $83 million to $57 million.

⚜

Jefferson oversaw the establishment of the United States Military Academy at West Point, which was founded on March 16, 1802, as part of the Military Peace Establishment Act. The Act also established new laws and limits for the military, bringing it firmly under the control of the civilian government. In 1805, the Jay Treaty expired, and he did nothing to renew it. He also pardoned a number of people who had been imprisoned under the Alien and Sedition Acts.

FIRST BARBARY WAR

❧

The Barbary States were nominally provinces of the Ottoman Empire, but they were independent countries. Tripoli, Algiers, Tunis and the Sultanate of Morocco fell under this umbrella title. The Barbary Coast of North Africa was rife with pirates, who were the scourge of the Mediterranean. It was estimated that from the 16th through the 19th centuries, the Barbary pirates kidnapped and enslaved some 1.25 million European citizens.

❧

While the States were still colonies, American shipping in the Mediterranean was protected from these pirates by the Royal Navy. These protections obviously fell away after independence, and as a result, the pirates began to attack American shipping. They captured American merchant ships, pillaged the goods in their holds, and kidnapped the crews, whom they later either ransomed or sold as slaves.

The first American ship to be attacked by the Barbary pirates was the *Betsey,* which was seized in October 1784. The Spanish government intervened and negotiated the release of the American men who had been taken a prisoner, and they advised the American government to pay tribute to the pirates in return for a cessation of future raids.

In 1785, Algerian pirates captured the American ships, *Maria* and *Dauphin*, enslaving 115 American sailors. Each of the four Barbary States demanded $600,000 for the release of the men. Unfortunately, the maximum budget that the American envoys had at that time was $40,000 to split among the Barbary States. Diplomacy failed to achieve any success, and the crews of these ships were to spend an entire decade in chains.

While he was still Minister to France, Jefferson sent envoys to Morocco and Algeria to attempt to negotiate treaties. Morocco signed a treaty with the United States on June 23, 1786, the first Barbary State to do so. Under that treaty, all piracy against American vessels was to cease, and any Americans captured by any of the Barbary States would be set free if they were to dock in any Moroccan city, to be protected by the Moroccan state. It was a diplomatic success.

Algeria was more of a problem. They were not interested in

ending their raids on American shipping. Jefferson and John Adams traveled to London in 1786 to negotiate with Tripoli's representative, Sidi Haji Abdrahaman. Abdrahaman stated that the Koran required all followers of the Prophet to plunder and enslave all people who were sinners, which, as non-Muslims, the American sailors were. The only solution, he advised, was more tribute. In 1795, Algeria offered to release the 115 American sailors in return for a tribute payment of $1 million, which at that time was fully one-sixth of the entire budget of the United States.

৩৯৩

Jefferson argued, and many came to agree, that giving in to the Barbary States' demands would only encourage the pirates to push for more tribute in the future. The United States Department of the Navy was created by an act of Congress in 1798. Just before Jefferson's inauguration, Congress passed an addendum that put six frigates under the direction of the President. These ships were to

> *"protect our commerce and chastise their (the Barbary*
> *States') insolence – by sinking, burning or*
> *destroying their ships and vessels wherever you*
> *shall find them."*

৩৯৩

After Jefferson was sworn in, Yusuf Karamanli, the Pasha of Tripoli, demanded $225,000 in tribute from the new administration. Jefferson refused. In retaliation, the Pasha declared war on the United States by cutting down the flagstaff in front of the U. S. Consulate in Tripoli. Algiers and Tunis did not join Tripoli in its declaration of war, and

Morocco continued to abide by its earlier treaty with the Americans.

⚜

In 1801, Jefferson ordered the United States Navy under Commodore Richard Dale to travel to the Mediterranean to make a show of force. This was the first time an American naval squadron crossed the Atlantic. The fleet engaged with the Barbary pirates, and after this first violent contact, Jefferson sought and was granted a declaration of war from Congress. It was the first foreign war fought by the United States.

⚜

Commodore Dale's fleet joined a Swedish fleet that was already blockading Tripoli, and the USS *Enterprise* vanquished the Barbary ship *Tripoli* in August 1801.

⚜

The Pasha of Tripoli, Yusuf Karamanli, allowed and possibly ordered a group of Barbary pirates to capture the USS *Philadelphia*. The United States Marines were able to take the ship back in a daring night raid. Jefferson sent the United States' Consul to Tunis, William Eaton, with a military force to topple Yusuf and place his brother on the throne. Eaton and a force of US Marines and 500 mercenaries marched from Alexandria, Egypt to Tripoli, where they captured the city of Derna. This victory was the first time the flag of the United States was raised on foreign soil.

⚜

With the threat of further military incursion by the Americans, and with the American blockade and bombardment of his city wearing his people down, Pasha Yusuf signed a peace treaty with the United States that restored peace to the Mediterranean, albeit temporarily. The people of the United States were overjoyed with the victory, and a monument was raised in the Washington Navy Yard. The Marine's Hymn includes a line about the shores of Tripoli in honor of the exploit.

LOUISIANA PURCHASE

❦

I n 1800, Spain ceded its ownership of the Louisiana territory to France. At the time, France was ruled by Napoleon Bonaparte, and Napoleon's interest in his new property posed a potential security risk to shipping on the Mississippi River and the United States as a whole.

❦

At Jefferson's behest, James Monroe and Robert Livingston went to Paris in 1803 to negotiate for the purchase of New Orleans and its adjacent coastal region, thereby placing the mouth of the Mississippi River firmly in American hands. Jefferson offered $10 million for a tract of land that was roughly 40,000 square miles.

❦

Much to the surprise of Monroe and Livingston, Napoleon

made a generous counteroffer. Realizing that his military had no way to hold such a large expanse of land and needing money to continue to prosecute his wars in Europe, the French leader offered to sell nearly 828,000 square miles of land for $15 million. This land purchase would effectively double the size of the United States. With limited time and communication across the Atlantic being such a lengthy proposition, the negotiators accepted Napoleon's offer and signed the treaty of sale on April 30, 1803.

⚜

Jefferson learned of his purchase on July 3, 1803. Although there were some concerns about the constitutionality of the federal government purchasing land, the Senate nevertheless voted to ratify the treaty on October 3, 1803.

⚜

There was great optimism about the purchase, and the land that was obtained turned out to be incredibly fertile, making the new nation self-sufficient in foodstuffs and other resources for the first time. The purchase also ended British and French military incursions into North America, and the way was opened for the westward expansion of the United States to begin.

EXPEDITIONS

❦

Jefferson knew that it was only a matter of time before settlers started pushing west into the new territory, and he wanted to know what he'd just bought. He also wanted to state a claim to the rumored Northwest Passage for the United States, hoping to head off the European powers who were seeking the same thing. Armed with the exploration accounts of Le Page du Pratz in Louisiana, published in 1763, he convinced Congress to fund an expedition to explore the continent all the way out to the Pacific Ocean.

❦

The Corps of Discovery was founded in 1803, and Jefferson tapped Merriweather Lewis and William Clark to be its leaders. He personally tutored Lewis on mapping, botany, natural history, mineralogy, astronomy, and navigation. He gave Lewis unlimited access to the library at Monticello, which at the time boasted the largest collection of books in the world on the natural history and geography of North America. He also had a sizeable collection of maps, which Lewis obviously found to be of great value.

☙❧

The Lewis and Clark Expedition lasted from May 1804 to September 1806 and returned with a wealth of information about the continent, significantly expanding knowledge and understanding of the geography, resources, and Native peoples of the land.

☙❧

Lewis and Clark were not the only explorers that Jefferson sent westward. He also sent William Dunbar and George Hunter to the Ouachita River in Arkansas and Louisiana; Thomas Freeman and Peter Custis to the Red River; and Zebulon Pike to the Rocky Mountains and the Southwest. Every expedition brought back valuable information, much to the delight of the eternally intellectually curious Jefferson.

NATIVE AMERICAN POLICIES

❧

J efferson's attitude toward Native Americans was as conflicted as his attitude toward blacks. He openly disputed with the popularly held belief that indigenous people were inferior to those of European descent, and he believed that they were in fact equal "***in body and mind***" to whites. That is where his magnanimity ended.

❧

As governor of Virginia, he advocated forcibly relocating the Cherokee and Shawnee tribes west of the Mississippi, allegedly because these tribes had supported the British during the Revolution. Once he became President, he arranged for Georgia to give up the lands it had claimed in the west in exchange for federal military assistance in clearing the Cherokee out of the state.

❧

He believed in assimilation and sought to "*civilize*" the Native Americans. He attempted to secure peace treaties with the tribes that encouraged them to adopt the American agricultural lifestyle and to relinquish their old ways. Many tribes accepted his proposal, but some opposed it. The Shawnee tribe split into two factions over the issue, with the side led by Black Hoof agreeing to Jefferson's policies and the other side, led by Tecumseh, actively and violently opposing them. Jefferson told Secretary of War General Henry Dearborn,

> *"If we are constrained to lift the hatchet against any tribe, we will never lay it down until that tribe is exterminated or driven beyond the Mississippi."*

❧ VI ❧
SECOND TERM

"Our country is now taking so steady a course as to show by what road it will pass to destruction, to wit: by consolidation of power first, and then corruption, its necessary consequence."

— THOMAS JEFFERSON

❧

Jefferson replaced Aaron Burr as his vice presidential candidate when he ran for re-election in 1804. His new running mate was George Clinton. Jefferson's relationship with Burr had been severely eroded by the outcome of the 1800 election, and Jefferson never stopped suspecting that Burr wanted the presidency for himself. In order to prevent Burr from gaining any sort of power base in Washington, Jefferson refused to appoint Burr's supporters to federal office, which infuriated Burr and opened a rift between them that would not heal.

CHALLENGES

৩ঌ

As soon as Jefferson was sworn in for his second term, he became involved in a political fracas with Supreme Court Justice Samuel Chase. Chase was a staunch Federalist, and he was unabashed in ruling in favor of his political allies. Jefferson determined to remove all Federalists from the bench, and he began by encouraging Congress to impeach Justice Chase. Virginia Congressman John Randolph and the House of Representatives served Chase with eight articles of impeachment based upon his judicial performance. The impeachment trial began in the Senate in 1805. Ultimately Chase was acquitted, Jefferson earned a permanent enemy in the form of Chief Justice John Marshall, and the proceedings raised constitutional questions regarding the independence of the judiciary. Although Chase was not convicted, his impeachment still helped to cement the idea that judges were prohibited from actively issuing rulings to further their partisan politics.

The Republican party suffered a serious rupture in March 1806, when fellow Virginian John Randolph accused Jefferson on the floor of the House of moving too far in a Federalist direction, betraying their party's political base. The split was hurtful, because Randolph was Jefferson's second cousin, and he had previously been a staunch ally. In 1808, Randolph and his companions found an extra reason to be alarmed when Jefferson became the first president to push for a federal building project aimed at constructing roads, bridges, and canals across several states.

Jefferson's popularity also was damaged by his response to events in Europe. He had a personal dislike for the British envoy, Anthony Merry, and this led to an erosion of previously positive relations between the two countries. Napoleon was waging a war of conquest in Europe, and after his victory at the Battle of Austerlitz, he unilaterally changed the terms of France's trade deals with the United States, and Jefferson's administration failed to counter these changes. Jefferson's response was the Embargo Act of 1807, which was aimed at goods from both France and Great Britain, but the end result was economic chaos at home. He abandoned the policy less than a year later.

The states had abolished the international slave trade during the revolution, but South Carolina reopened in 1806. Jefferson decried this action in a December 1806 speech, calling on Congress to criminalize the international slave trade through federal legislation. In accordance with his wishes, Congress passed the Act Prohibiting Importation of Slaves, which Jefferson signed into law in 1807. The act barred international slave trading, but it did nothing to address the trade within the United States.

AARON BURR

꧁꧂

I n 1804, shortly after he was dumped from the Democratic-Republican ticket, Aaron Burr suffered a drubbing at the polls when he ran for governor of New York. During the campaign, Alexander Hamilton had made inflammatory comments in public about the nature of Burr's character, and so Burr challenged Hamilton to a duel. On July 11, 1804, Burr shot and killed Hamilton. He was indicted for murder in New York and New Jersey, so he fled to Georgia. At about the same time, he was approached by New England separatists who wanted him to lead them in a New England Federation. They quickly distanced themselves from Burr after Hamilton's demise, and the still-sitting vice president's reputation and business dealings suffered. Looking for a way to improve his lot, he approached British ambassador Anthony Merry and offered to capture territory in the western United States in return for money and British ships.

꧁꧂

After his term as vice president ended, Burr traveled to Louisiana and began to conspire with the territorial governor, James Wilkinson. They began to recruit for a military expedition with the help of additional conspirators Senator John Smith of Ohio and an Irishman named Harmon Blennerhassett. During this time period, Burr floated a number of ideas that ranged from having New Orleans secede to create its state to invading and conquering Mexico or Spanish Florida. The ideas he came up with were many and varied, and to this day, nobody really knows what his goal really was.

※

In Fall 1806, Burr and a flotilla of ships with approximately sixty men set sail down the Ohio River toward New Orleans. At this point, Governor Wilkinson turned on him and reported Burr's activities to Jefferson, who immediately ordered his arrest. Burr was finally caught in Bayou Pierre, a wild area in Louisiana, and on February 13, 1807, he was sent to Virginia to stand trial for treason.

※

Burr's trial was a circus. Jefferson tried to influence the verdict by proclaiming Burr's obvious guilt in a speech before Congress. When the case actually came to trial, the judge was John Marshall, the Supreme Court Justice who was a political foe of Jefferson's, and he dismissed all charges. Burr's lawyers attempted to subpoena Jefferson to testify, but he invoked executive privilege and refused. This was the first exercise of executive privilege in the American presidency.

※

The trial lasted for three months, ultimately resulting in Burr's acquittal. Jefferson was furious and denounced the verdict. He removed Wilkinson from his position as governor but permitted him to retain his military commission.

THE CHESAPEAKE-LEOPARD
AFFAIR

֎

Throughout 1806 and 1807, the British Navy's press gangs busily raided American merchant ships and press-ganged their crews into service with the Royal Navy. Diplomacy did nothing to stop the impressment of American sailors, and Britain continued to harass American shipping.

֎

In June 1807, the HMS *Leopard* hailed the USS *Chesapeake* off the coast of Virginia. The commander of the American vessel, Commodore James Barron, accepted Lieutenant John Meade from the *Leopard*, and upon his arrival, Meade served Barron with a search warrant. The British, he claimed, were looking for deserters from the Royal Navy. After a brief discussion, Meade returned to the *Leopard*, and British Captain Humphreys demanded that the Americans surrender. The Americans declined, and the *Leopard* fired broadsides into the *Chesapeake*. Three of the crew were killed, and 18 were injured, including Barron. Completely unprepared for battle, Barron had no choice but to surrender. Humphreys refused the capitulation and boarded the *Chesapeake*, seizing four Royal Navy deserters, three of whom were American citizens. The British citizen was hanged from the yardarm of the HMS *Halifax*, and the three Americans were sentenced to 500 lashes each. The sentences were commuted.

Jefferson was furious. He issued a proclamation banning British ships from American waters and called on the states to call up 100,000 men and the materiel to arm them. The USS *Revenge* was sent to demand an explanation from the British government, but when it, too, was fired upon, Jefferson called a special session of Congress to discuss either an embargo of British goods or a declaration of war.

In December, Napoleon announced an embargo of British goods, preventing Britain from legally conducting any commerce in Europe, which was largely under Napoleon's control at that time. In response, George III ordered the impressment of American sailors to be intensified. Congress, in turn, passed the Embargo Act, which prohibited all British goods.

The embargo was not what one might call a success. The American economy suffered, and smugglers and scofflaws began to sell British goods at high prices on the black market.

Jefferson sent federal agents to track down and apprehend these smugglers. There was no real way to prevent American merchants from importing foreign goods, especially since they could just sail into international waters to conduct their business, but exports were sharply curtailed. The embargo failed.

⚜

Another unintended consequence of the Embargo Act was Jefferson, who had always been against centralization of power, found himself expanding federal authority at the expense of the states. It was an untenable position politically, and the economic difficulties caused by the embargo helped to return the Federalists to power.

⚜

In December 1807, Jefferson announced that he had no intention of seeking a third term and he retired to Monticello. Although he was still President, he left the actual affairs of state and business of running the country almost entirely to James Madison and Treasury Secretary Gallatin. Just before he left office in 1809, Jefferson repealed the disastrous embargo.

⚜

Shortly after Madison's inauguration as his successor, Jefferson said that he felt like a prisoner who had been released from his chains.

63

❧ VII ❧

RETURN TO PRIVATE LIFE

"I tremble for my country when I reflect that God I just; that his justice cannot sleep forever."

— THOMAS JEFFERSON

༻⚜༺

During the years immediately after his time as President ended, Jefferson turned to his first love: education and learning. He sold his extensive book collection to the Library of Congress and began to correspond with the country's leaders. He advised James Monroe on westward expansion, and many see Jefferson's fingerprints on the famous Monroe Doctrine of 1823.

༻⚜༺

Jefferson happily developed a routine. He would rise early, spend several hours reading and writing his copious correspondence, and in the afternoon he would oversee his plantation from horseback. In the evenings, he would spend time with his family in the garden, and then go to bed late at night with a book. He would have been happy to live his life just this way, with only his family around him, but his peace and quiet was frequently interrupted by visitors and even tourists who called without warning. He complained that Monticello had become a "*virtual hotel,*" but he never turned anyone away.

UNIVERSITY OF VIRGINIA

❧

Jefferson had never been a religious man, and he believed that the key to a successful society was education without the interference or influence of any church. He wanted a university where students from all walks of life could study any topic they chose, where their studies would be publicly funded, and they could enroll based on ability rather than social class or wealth.

❧

In 1819, at the age of 70, Jefferson founded the University of Virginia. He organized a campaign in the state legislature for its charter, and he purchased the land for the university with the assistance of Edmund Bacon. He designed most of the buildings, planned the curriculum, and acted as the school's first rector when the university opened its doors in 1825.

❧

Like most of Jefferson's architecture, the buildings at the University of Virginia were based on Greek and Roman structures. The university library, called the Rotunda, was based upon the Roman Pantheon, and each academic unit was designed with a two-story façade in the form of a columned Greek temple. The Rotunda was the center of the campus, which was a controversial thing at the time – all other universities were centered on churches. The university was always meant to be a secular institution.

⚜

The standard university education at that time had three possible areas of focus: medicine, law or divinity. Under the Jefferson's direction, the University of Virginia had eight separate and independent schools: medicine, law, mathematics, chemistry, ancient languages, modern languages, natural philosophy and moral philosophy. These were all areas where Jefferson himself was skilled.

⚜

Jefferson hosted dinners at Monticello on Sundays for faculty and students for the rest of his life. When Jefferson passed away, he bequeathed the majority of his library to the university.

JEFFERSON AND ADAMS

❧

There have rarely been two politicians as entwined throughout their careers as Thomas Jefferson and John Adams. They began as good friends when they served in the Continental Congress together and then again when they represented the United States' interests in Europe. Party politics shattered their friendship, and after Jefferson's election to the presidency, the two men were not on speaking terms for more than ten years.

❧

In 1804, when Jefferson's daughter Polly passed away, Abigail Adams wrote to Jefferson and attempted to arrange reconciliation, but when the men did write to one another again, their old arguments flared up, and they became hostile once more.

❧

Benjamin Rush, another signer of the Declaration of Independence, was dedicated to healing the rift between the two men. He prodded them continually to contact one another, and his efforts combined with the passage of time led to Adams sending a New Year's letter to Jefferson. Jefferson responded with warmth, which prompted Adams to write back. The two began a 14-year correspondence during which they exchanged 158 letters debating politics, history, and the impact of the American revolution on the world.

ॐ

When Adams died, his last words were, "***Thomas Jefferson survives.***" Unfortunately, in an extraordinary coincidence, Jefferson had actually died a few hours before.

AUTOBIOGRAPHY

❧

In 1821, when he was 77 years old, Jefferson put pen to paper and began writing an autobiography. He focused exclusively on the years of the revolution, excluding his boyhood and youth. He wrote about nothing that happened after July 29, 1790.

❧

Jefferson had never been particularly interested in his family history, but he did write that his family had come to the New World from Wales, settling in Virginia in the late 17th Century. He described his father as a good man with a strong mind and sound judgment despite the fact that he was uneducated. After these basic sketches, he concentrated on the Declaration of Independence and the establishment of the state government of Virginia.

❧

He took the opportunity to express his opinions and insights about human nature, politics, and historical events. He decried the aristocracy of landowners, saying that he would rather see an aristocracy of talent and virtue. Jefferson also stated that he felt his personal affairs were unimportant and best if overlooked.

LAFAYETTE

❧

When he left Paris in 1789, Jefferson had parted from his good friend the Marquis de Lafayette. The two had written to one another, but they had not seen each other in many, many years. In 1824, Lafayette accepted an invitation from President James Monroe to visit the United States to see what he had helped to create. He visited New York, New England, and Washington, but when his official visits were done, Lafayette went to Monticello.

❧

The visit was an emotional one for them both. Jefferson's grandson, Randolph, described how the two men burst into tears and embraced when they saw one another. Lafayette stayed at Monticello for 11 days, during which he, Jefferson and President Monroe toured the University of Virginia and attended a banquet. Jefferson had prepared a speech for the occasion, but his voice was weak, so he had someone else read it for him. It was his last public appearance.

SUNSET

❦

In his final years, Jefferson was deeply indebted, to the tune of $100,000. He worried about making good on this debt, especially as he realized that his life was coming to an end and he would have little to leave to his heirs. He applied to the General Assembly of Virginia to hold a public lottery as a fundraiser, and the Assembly consented.

❦

His health began to fail in 1825, a combination of disorders of the intestines and urinary tract, rheumatism, and old and painful injuries of the wrist and arms. He was confined to bed in June 1826, and on July 4, at 12:50 pm, Jefferson died at the age of 83. The date of his death was the 50th anniversary of the Declaration of Independence, and it was also, as previously mentioned, the date of John Adams' demise.

❦

When he died, a golden locket was found around Jefferson's neck. It contained a lock of his wife Martha's hair, bound by a faded blue ribbon.

⚜

At the time of his death, Jefferson was still deeply in debt, and though he left instructions for the disposition of his estate and the emancipation of Sally Hemings' children, the estate was sold at public auction in 1827. His possessions and slaves were all sold to pay off his expenses, and in 1831, his heirs sold Monticello.

❧ VIII ❧
LEGACY

"When a man assumes a public trust, he should consider himself a public property."

— THOMAS JEFFERSON

❧

Thomas Jefferson was one of the most influential political philosophers of his day. He had marked opinions, and his persuasive writing ensured that his influence would continue to be felt long after his death.

GOVERNMENT

❦

His vision of government based upon ideals of political equality is known as *"Jeffersonian democracy."* Jefferson strongly believed that each individual was born with *"certain inalienable rights,"* which included liberty up until the moment that liberty infringed on the rights of others. He was also a staunch supporter of the separation of church and state. He distrusted cities and bankers, and he believed that tyranny was an outgrowth of corruption in politics and monarchies. He was opposed to centralization of power, which informed his support for states' rights.

❦

At the time of his death, the United States was the only existing republic in an age of monarchies. Jefferson was a tireless opponent of monarchies and hereditary power, and he opined that frequent small outbreaks of rebellion and revolution were necessary to keep monarchies, governments and other powerful entities in check. He believed that the majority of human history was a tale of a majority oppressed by a powerful minority, and he believed in democracy as pure majority rule.

⚜

Jefferson believed in public education and freedom of the press. He also supported the idea of providing the vote not just to landholders but also to laborers who did not own land. He wanted to increase voter participation, and while his party was in power, this did indeed happen. He was displeased that the vote was largely in the hands of rich and powerful landowners, believing that this was an echo of the feudal system of monarchy. He wanted to expand suffrage to include *"**yeoman farmers,**"* but he excluded tenant farmers, day laborers, vagrants, most Native Americans, and women. It was his belief that voting should be restricted only to those people who were free of outside influences and corrupting dependence on other people or institutions.

⚜

While he was a firm believer in democracy, he realized that there would be times when there would be failures or excesses. These would be the fault of corrupt institutions rather than the foibles of human nature, which separated him from some of his more cynical compatriots who doubted if human beings could be trusted to govern themselves.

80

RELIGION

❦

J efferson was baptized into the Episcopal Church, but after being influenced by Deists and studying the New Testament on his own, he broke from traditional Christianity. He called himself a Christian,

"in the only sense in which Jesus wished anyone to be."

He compiled all of Jesus's words and teachings, omitting all references to the miracles or the supernatural, and created *The Life and Morals of Jesus of Nazareth*, which is known today as the *Jefferson Bible*.

❦

He strongly disliked priests and clergy of all kinds, and he toyed with the idea of banning all members of the clergy from public office. He believed that the clergy, dedicated to the hierarchies of their respective churches, were the enemies of liberty and discouraged individual liberty in favor of conformity. He drafted the Virginia Statute of Religious Freedom, which was ratified in 1786, and he was so proud of this accomplishment that it was only one of his voluminous writings to be included in the epitaph he wrote for his gravestone.

☙❧

Jefferson hoped that the American people would be educated in multiple faiths and would create an "*Apiarian*" religion, which meant that the people would rationally take the best features of every religion and discard the rest. He believed in a Creator and an afterlife, but he denied the divinity of Jesus and rejected the concept of the Trinity. These beliefs were extremely controversial in their time, and they featured strongly in opposition to his election for a second term as President.

☙❧

During the campaign for the 1800 election, the *New England Palladium* referred to Jefferson as an "*infidel,*" and the Federalists called him a "*howling atheist.*" He never denied the existence of or his belief in God, but the opposition to his views that he experienced during that campaign led him to become more reticent to discuss his beliefs in public.

BANKS

✣✣✣

He was always a farmer at heart, and he believed that agrarian citizens were hurt in the long run by government banks and public borrowing. He believed that such institutions encouraged risk-taking, long-term debt, monopolies and dangerous financial speculation. He disliked Alexander Hamilton primarily because his rival was a staunch supporter of a national bank, and that friction was the seed of all the acrimony between them.

✣✣✣

Jefferson and Madison both felt that a national bank would be neglectful to the needs of individuals and farmers. Jefferson also believed that the foundation of a national bank would violate the Tenth Amendment and would be a violation of states' rights. He wanted to abolish the national bank when he became President, and only the efforts of Secretary of the

Treasury Albert Gallatin convinced him to let the bank remain.

SLAVERY

❧

Thomas Jefferson was a slave owner, which was a dreadful contradiction for a man who so frequently stated his belief in personal liberty. Over his lifetime, he owned over 600 human beings. He inherited 175 of these people, and the rest were born into bondage on his plantations. While he may have been a benevolent slaveholder, the fact remains that he continually denied personal liberty to the people who worked his land while he sat in Monticello and wrote vaunted words about liberty and freedom.

❧

He felt that slavery was harmful to everyone involved with it, both slave and master, but he never saw fit to distance himself from it completely. His personal wealth, based as it was on the plantation system, depended upon slave labor to be maintained. At the same time, he frequently included verbiage highly critical to the institution of slavery in his writings. Passages calling for the abolition of slavery were included in, but later struck from, the Declaration of Independence.

❦

He believed, as many white men of his time did, that blacks were inherently inferior to whites both mentally and physically. Despite this, he also believed that they had innate rights that should not be violated. In *Notes on the State of Virginia*, he called slavery a moral evil and stated that the United States would one day be called to account by God. He supported freeing slaves, but immediately deporting them to Liberia or Sierra Leone. He did not believe that whites and blacks could live together as free members of the same society, and following the slave revolt in Haiti, he feared a race war in America.

❦

Jefferson was allegedly a benevolent slaveholder. He purchased slaves to reunite families, but he also sold about 110 slaves to obtain funds. By the standards of the day, he didn't force his slaves to work on Sundays or Christmas, and he allowed them personal time during the winter. He provided them with log cabins with fireplaces, good, clothing and household goods, and he gave them financial incentives for jobs well done. He also allowed them to raise their chickens and to grow gardens. His nail factory was operated by child slaves, but these same slaves went on to become craftsmen, and he frequently promoted slaves to better positions on the plantation.

❦

Benevolence as a slaveholder, however, is still an offense to the personhood and liberty of the slave, and in a way, saying Jefferson was a "***good master***" is damning with faint praise.

THE SALLY HEMINGS QUESTION

❦

I n 1802, a man named James Callender was denied the position of postmaster. He immediately retaliated by proclaiming in public that Jefferson had taken slave Sally Hemings as "*a concubine*" and that she had borne him several children. This allegation was dismissed by polite society, but it was an open secret that many slave owners had children with women they enslaved.

❦

Sally Hemings was the daughter of John Wayles, Jefferson's father-in-law, and Betty Hemings, Wayles "*mulatto*" slave. She was his wife Martha's half-sister and was three-quarters European and one-quarter African.

❦

Jefferson's family denied the relationship, but visitors to

Monticello often remarked on the close resemblance of the Hemings children to Jefferson himself. Randolph Jefferson, Thomas's grandson, once claimed that the last Peter Carr, Jefferson's nephew by his sister, had fired Hemings' children, but this claim was never credited.

⚘

In 1794, Jefferson freed his slave Robert Hemings, and in 1796, he also freed James Hemings, who was his cook. A slave named Harriet Hemings was freed in 1822 when she tried to run away, and in his will, he freed five more male slaves named Hemings.

⚘

Sally had four children who survived to adulthood: William Beverly, Harriet, Madison and Eston Hemings. All but Madison identified themselves as white and lived in white communities. In 1873, Madison Hemings went on record in an Ohio newspaper stating that Jefferson was his father. He claimed that all of his siblings were Jefferson's children, and that claim was backed by Israel Jefferson, another freed slave who had worked at Monticello. Madison was dismissed as a liar.

⚘

The rumor would not go away, something that plagued Jefferson's descendants. Mainstream historians gave no credence to the story, but African-American historians kept the story alive. Finally, in 1998, a DNA study was conducted on the Y-chromosome of a direct male-line descendant of Eston Hemings. It was found to be a nearly perfect match to

89

descendants of Jefferson's paternal uncle. Peter Carr's descendants were not a match to the Hemings sample. The results of this test were interpreted as stating with 99% certainty that Jefferson was indeed the father of Sally Hemings' children.

☙❧

In July 2017, the Thomas Jefferson Foundation announced that archaeologists who were excavating at Monticello had located what they believed were Sally Hemings' quarters, adjacent to Jefferson's bedchamber. This chamber has been preserved as part of the Mountaintop Project, which is dedicated to the restoration of Monticello. Tours of Monticello now include acknowledgment of Jefferson's relationship with Hemings.

☙❧

Sally Hemings was never emancipated. She was, however, permitted by Jefferson's daughter Patsy to live with her freed sons as a free woman in Charlottesville, Virginia. She died in 1835.

❧ IX ❧

THE MEASURE OF A MAN

"I was bold in the pursuit of knowledge, never fearing to follow truth and reason to whatever results they led, and bearding every authority which stood in their way."

— THOMAS JEFFERSON

❧

Thomas Jefferson is remembered today as an icon of personal liberty, democracy, republicanism and as one of the Founding Fathers whose efforts brought the United States into being. He was more than a politician, and his contributions to American society are nothing less than staggering.

❧

He was a true Renaissance man. He was a member of the American Philosophical Society for 35 years and served as the president of that organization for 18 years. He was a scientist, fascinated by the development of new crops and scientific agricultural techniques. He was an architect who helped to promote the popularity of neo-classical and Neo-Palladian architectural forms. He was a prodigious writer, a linguist who mastered several languages, and a naturalist who studied birds, wine, natural bridges and soil conditions. He designed gardens and invented the swivel chair, the prototype of which he used while he was writing the Declaration of Independence. He improved many contemporary inventions, adapting them to his needs. These inventions included the pedometer, the polygraph (not the lie detector, but a device that duplicated writing), the revolving bookcase and a form of plow called the moldboard plow.

୧୬୨

His strong support of states' rights caused him to lose popularity during the Civil War years, and his contradictory record on human rights, particularly slavery, have dimmed his luster over the years. Despite this, he was named as the fifth greatest President the country ever had in a 2015 Brookings Institution poll of the American Political Science Association.

୧୬୨

Thomas Jefferson was a complex individual, with good qualities and bad qualities, as most people have. His accomplishments may be blemished by his failings, but he stands out as one of the most remarkable men of his day.

❧ X ❧
BIBLIOGRAPHY

෨෯෨

- Bernstein, Richard B. (2003). *Thomas Jefferson.*
  Oxford University Press. ISBN 978-0195181302.
- Bober, Natalie (2008). *Thomas Jefferson: Draftsman
  of a Nation.* University of Virginia Press. ISBN 978-
  0813927329.
- Cogliano, Francis D (2008). *Thomas Jefferson:
  Reputation and Legacy.* Edinburgh University Press.
  ISBN 978-0748624997.
- Meacham, Jon (2012). *Thomas Jefferson: The Art of
  Power.* Random House LLC. ISBN 978-
  0679645368.
- Randall, Willard Sterne (1994). *Thomas Jefferson: A
  Life.* Harper Collins. ISBN 0060976179.

YOUR FREE EBOOK!

As a way of saying thank you for reading our book, we're offering you a free copy of the below eBook.

Happy Reading!